Black White
~ and ~
Mocha Cream

Poems

A N G E L A   M A R I E

authorHOUSE®

AuthorHouse™
1663 Liberty Drive
Bloomington, IN 47403
www.authorhouse.com
Phone: 1 (800) 839-8640

Published by AuthorHouse   06/29/2015

ISBN: 978-1-5049-2080-3
ISBN: 978-1-5049-2081-0

Library of Congress Control Number: 2015910430

Print information available on the last page.

Any people depicted in stock imagery provided by Thinkstock are models,
and such images are being used for illustrative purposes only.
Certain stock imagery © Thinkstock.

This book is printed on acid-free paper.

Contents

***Dedicated** to My **Loving** Husband James,*

*My **Delightful** son Josiah,*

To Mommy, Daddy, Alfred, and Stephen

To Joshua, Alyssa, Brandon, Tylar, Aunt Sue, and Aunt Diane…

***To Everyone** that took the time to listen to my words,*

*To Everyone that took the time to listen to the
poise and position of my thoughts…*

***To Anyone** that was a part of my life near, far, present or past….*

***Because for me**…*

It takes a village to write a book…

It takes multiple seasons to write…

*It takes family, friends, coworkers, associates, passers by,
experiences, and observations **to grow, love, and write**…*

About the Author

Angela Marie is an inspired writer. She is an artist of words. She is a mother and wife. She has been an educator of children and has worked in public education for over twenty years. She attended Temple University for her undergraduate degree and Grand Canyon University for her graduate work. She is a Christian and desires to uplift, encourage, and lead human kind toward a sober and sound emotional state. She is a product of the Philadelphia Public School System and resides in Philadelphia. She is an intense observer. Angela is an empathetic conversationalist and has painted with words since she was a teenager.

Painful Lessons

by Angela Marie
Written 3/14/2009 @ 7:25 PM

I have to teach my son
My African American Boy…

The velvet
The richness
The soil of who he is…

I have to demonstrate
Confidence
And
Assurance of the ability of his mind
Because all of America isn't all kind…

I have to remind him of attire he can't wear
Because hooded jackets for warmth
Are dangerous
Somewheres…

Rules he must follow
And exactly…
Because profiling
Is real for my Black brothers
Especially.

I'll direct him toward college
And he shall succeed and exceed

But the ills of
Profiling
And prejudices
Is
Painful
For
Me
To teach.

Tender Faces

by Angela Marie
Written March 7, 2008

I've looked into many tender faces and
And vibrant minds...

Praying and hoping for great things to come to full fruition.

Prisons for them,
I don't foresee...

But college and entrepreneurs
And financial stability.

I've looked into many tender faces
And vibrant minds...

Praying and hoping for great things to come to full fruition.

Drugs, prostitution, and abuse
I don't foresee...

But vocation, family and love
Is what the human heart seeks

I've looked into many tender faces
And vibrant minds....
I've come to realize that the children need to be taught
Values and life's oughts and naughts.

I've looked into many tender faces and vibrant minds and I've come to
realize…
That children need teachers…

I've come to realize that children need redirection.
I've come to realize that the children need hopes and dreams.
I've come to realize that the children need wholesome love.

I don't see young brown faces and their demise…

I see vibrant minds.
I see a positive nation on the rise.
I see hopes and dreams…
I see great things coming to full fruition.

I see great things coming to full fruition.
I see great things coming to full fruition.

Colored Chile Beware

by Angela Marie
Written July 13, 2009 @ 10:32 a.m.

Emancipation Proclamation
Henceforth and for evermore

Jim Crow
And his descendants lay dormant
In sepulchers
In cardiac arrest

He spoke today.

Segregation and his insidious secrets
Lay hidden beneath the nook of venomous tongues...

Spoke today.
jim crow danced today.
Awakened some
And killed more
Colored young...
Lynching liberated dreams
And all that equality and pursuits bring...

jim crow danced today
and spat in colored faces
as before.

Removing the scales
Painted naïve and optimistic eyes and obscured perception...

Rusted chains of iron…
Roped necks, hand, and feet today.

Beware.
Jim Crow lurks.
The faint heart of klan…
Burning crosses on colored land.
Suited ties
Eloquent speech and the venom beneath…
A slow poison…

Beware
And know the dangers of jim crow.
Beware and know that he's in the educational institution you seek.
He's in the boardroom
Professional and sleek.

Colored Chile,
Continue to prosper, excel and succeed
The Holy
Ghost will carry you with safety upon His wings.

Be cognizant
And know
About the ugliness of jim crow.

Be cognizant
And know
About the ugliness of jim crow.
And continue to prosper, excel, and grow,
Dear
Colored
Chile.

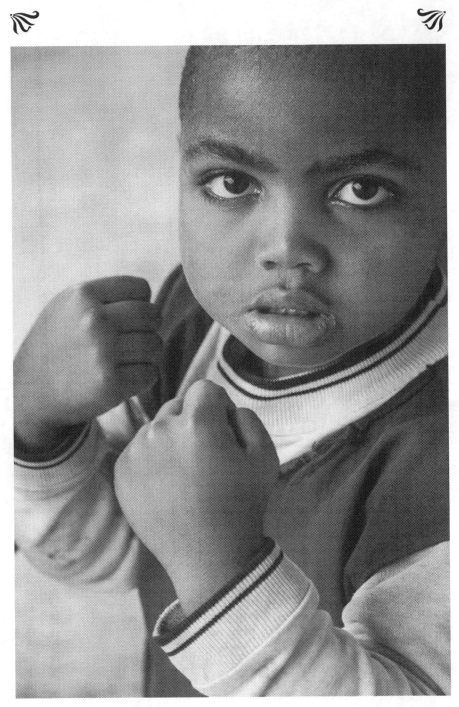

From A Boy

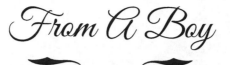

by Angela Marie

Dear Teacher,

My name is Boy

I want to learn,
Just don't redirect me…
Just teach me as I am…

Young and vulnerable…

I'm hurting
I'm in pain
Mommy took that glass pipe and inhaled…
Mommy nodded, nodded, nodded…
And I cried for milk…

Mommy nodded, nodded, nodded…

I want to learn
Just don't redirect me…
Just teach me as I am…

Young and Vulnerable…

I'm angry
But I don't know that I am…
Don't know what I am…
Don't know who I am…

Just teach me as I am…

Young and vulnerable…

Mommy nodded, nodded, nodded…

I'm hurting
I'm in pain
But I don't know that I am…
Don't know what I am…
Don't know who I am…

I cried for milk…

Mommy nodded, nodded, nodded…

I want to learn…
Just teach me as I am…

I flip tables
And cuss in your face…
I reach down in my pant and masturbate…

I cuss and fight anyone that looks at me
Bigger than me
Smaller than me

Anyone that appears to bother me
Real or imagined…

I want to learn…
Really I do…

Just teach me as I am…

Young and Vulnerable…

I'm angry
But I don't know that I am…
Don't know what I am…
Don't know who I am…

Just teach me how to read.
Just teach me how to count.
Just teach me how to speak…

I'm sorry for flipping the tables…
I 'm sorry for punching the teachers and students in the face…

Just teach me…
As I am…

Young and vulnerable…

I'm angry
I'm hurting

Will the system nod on me too…
Will the teacher nod on me too.

The Love of Learning

by Angela Marie
Written January, 2008

Wisdom and I became friends...
Walking up and down the street, the halls, the mountains and valleys.

Each book that I read
Each language that I navigate
Is a gem to me.

We've had loud and silent conversations abut the importance of learning.

I thirst and love the elements of gaining knowledge.
I thirst and love the dynamics of imbibing information into my very
vein...

Each drop of history
Each angle of geometry
Is a gem to me...

We've had loud and silent conversations about the importance of
learning.

I thirst and love learning...
Because it prepared me for life...
I thirst and love learning because it teaches me to maneuver when facing
episodes of
Sadness, discomfort, or strife.

Each inference that I make
Each application of formula that I see
Is a gem to me.

I thirst and love learning…
Because it scaffolds my thinking
And prepares me for every situation…

I am able to articulate my thoughts
And examine them before I speak…

Knowledge is a gem to me…

Wisdom tells me to listen to the insights whispered in poetry
Wisdom tells me to pay attention to the events and repetitions of history.

Learning is a gem to me.
Knowledge is a gem to me.
Cognitive development is an ongoing desire
It is the fire of life.
Wisdom is a friend to me.

Torn Tapestry

by Angela Marie
Written 3/15/2009 @5:25 PM

Katrina
Regina
Michelle
Short hair
Ponytails
With
Smooth and beautiful browned skin…
African beauties
With out and within
  Filled with wit
    And confidence
      Their gain

Puddin'
Light skinned
Long hair
America's beauty and wit
    Her gain

Beauty and strength
Both different but the same

Young and hopeful

The trio of chocolate harassed and hated Puddin' because of her
creeeeeeeaaaammy
Skin

Not because of the intellect or any conversation with them

This trio of chocolate looked at Puddin' with disdain and hatred
They provoked her to fight with and fist
Tauntings and hauntings and jeerings
Persist
Persisted
Still
Exist

Puddin' had to learn to fight during her elementary years
An uneasy plight

I saw and see her tears

Both Puddin' and the beautiful trio are photos of tapestry to behold

This house and field slave confrontation is old…

Brown and light
Perspectives of beauty

Battles between the hues and textures of hair within our race
Why not embrace
Our differences

This prejudice within a race is old
I mean before Puddin' and the trio were born…

This fabric needs and needed mending…
It's torn
It leaves me forlorn and ripped inside
Resonating a theme of blue
And
All
Its
Hue

Answer Me

by Angela Marie
Written 8/22/2008 2 11:16 a.m.

This poem was written in response to conversations about learning
about cultures.

Yes, I am privileged
  And white
    And quietly learning
      About injustices
        Or minority culture
          Especially African Americans.

I'm ashamed
  I'm embarrassed
    That we placed people of color in chains
      And my ignorance
        Voiced blame to Black Folks
          For their anger
            Aggression
              Lack of education
And lack of CEO gain.

I'm trying to learn
And I have questions to ask
So, please don't get weary of my constant inquiry.

Don't say to me
"Don't you get it?
Don't ask anymore"

Be patient with White skinned and privileged me
I want to grow and explore.

Yes, I'm White and teaching Brown children
I'm falling in love with them as me
And learning to understand the culture and history...

So, don't say to me
"Don't you get it?
Don't ask anymore"

Be patient with White skinned and privileged me
I want to grow and explore.

Please don't ignore my innocent and sincere plea...

Sincerely,
Jane

In Reply

by Angela Marie
Written 2008 this poem is to be read in response
to the poem, Answer Me, by Angela Marie

Dear Jane
I hear what you are saying
But are you ready to understand the nuance of my world?

If you and
Not I
Take the scales off your eyes
Without my explaining
You'll understand why…

Read a book
By James Baldwin
Or Richard Wright's Native Son
Or view the Civil Rights movement
And
The
Still
Animalistic treatment
Done and done
And
Done and done

Imagine performing at the theatre
And you're the money makin' star of the show
But the entrance of the back door is where you **must** go…

Imagine being told of your ignorance
Just because of the color of your face.

Dear Jane
Dear Jane
There are challenges I face.
    Are you ready to understand my world?
        The worldwide abuse?
           Are you ready to learn that some of your truths about us are
           untrue?

We can talk
I agree to that
But don't be afraid of some hard hitting facts…

If you
And
Not I
Take the scales off your eyes
Without my explaining you will understand why…

Read a book
By James Baldwin
Or Richard Wright's Native Son
Or
View the Civil Rights Movement
And learn about my people
And learn about the ills done to my people
And understand the struggle of my people
And appreciate the jewel of my people

Read a book
By James Baldwin
Or the history of Harriet Tubman
Poems by Phyllis Wheatly
And some thinking will take place
Some new
Some undone

Sincerely,

Buster

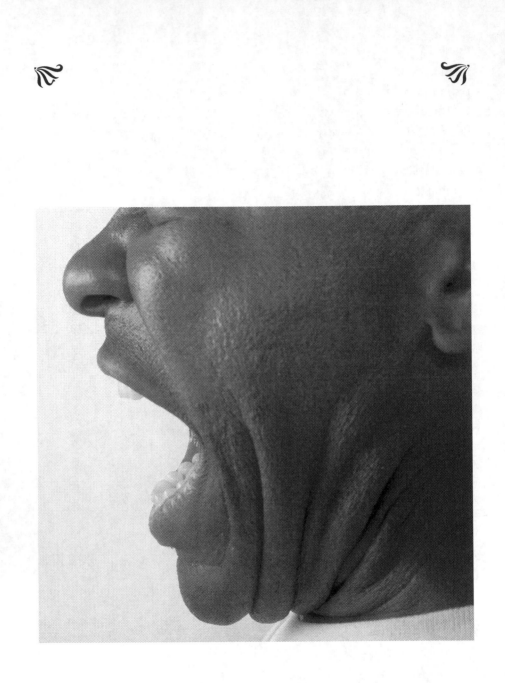

Just Hear My Angst

by Angela Marie

Just hear my oppression
Just understand my voice
That
Assigned names
Like nigger
   Sambo
      And
         Mammy
           Were not my choice

        Just hear my frustration
         Just understand my angst
          That
           Iron chains
            And unwanted criticism
            Was predetermined
           By another
              Privileged and dominant race

Sometimes I'm afraid of lynching
   Physically and institutionally
      I want to close my eyes and be treated like a human being.

It's a sensitive subject
And I'm assimilating along
But please don't ignore
Prejudicial
Ills
And
Wrongs

Just hear my frustration
Just understand my angst

This racial tension is LOUD
But I wish it
Ain't

But It Wasn't Always so...

by Angela Marie
written 6/27/2015 @ 12:41 a.m.

I woke up this mornin' with my mind stayed on Jesus....
But it wasn't always so....
That wasn't the always the case...

There was a war going on inside my brain...
This thinking place...

Thinking of things that ought not be...
Blasphemous things ...
But oh the King of Glory!!!
He stepped right in! He stepped right in!!
Flooding my mind....
Of His actions to protect my mind...
The finished work at the cross....
That's what HE did for me!!!
Making an open shame, of Satan, the enemy!

I woke up this mornin' with my mind stayed on Jesus...
But it wasn't always so...
That wasn't always the case...

Oh I thought about love and the he, that man….. I grew to hate…
But Oh the King of Glory!!!
Jesus stepped right in! He stepped right in!!
      Flooding my mind…
      Of HIS Resurrection Power…
      HE wouldn't let my heart, my mind grow sour!
      That's what HE did for me!!!
Giving me Triumph in HIS Triumph!
I couldn't fight for me!!
You see…

I woke up this mornin' with my mind stayed on Jesus…
And I PRAISE HIM!!!
And I PRAISE HIM!!!
Because it wasn't always so…
I was always presented with some reason, to hold my head low…

And I realize, that I am not a Queen or fabric of His royalty to merely flaunt
But to spread HIS love and Deliverance…

With Nobility
Comes responsibility…
Sober thinking and talking and in the places that I go…

I woke up this mornin' with my mind stayed on Jesus…
Hallelu!   Hallelu!   Halleluiah!

Laced with Grace ...
A Purged Brothel...

by Angela Marie written 6/29/2012 @ 11:15a.m.

I've been
    A provocative tease
        An alluring adulterous…
            Short hair
                Long hair
                    Smart and dumb…
                        I've been whatever
                          The he…
                              Wanted me to be…
                                  And that's what I'd become…

Exposing parts
    That should be kept secret
        And protected…
            And…
                The he…
                    Played with me
                        Privately…

Then,
    He'd shun, reject, and grope me with disrespect…
        And hurl attitudes of vomit
            At my heart and breast…

All I really wanted
    Was acceptance…

            Affirmation…
                Beauty…
                    And accented love…
Instead, I gained disdained disgrace
    From the circle of friends and family I embraced…
I'd cry…fall forlorn on my face…
Until one day…
I received God's undeserved…
Vast…
Grace…

His mercy…
Do you believe?
His Son Jesus
And Holy Spirit
I received?

The Holy Spirit revealed to me…
That Jesus Christ
Died for
Tainted

Dung smeared me…

The Holy Spirit revealed to me…
That Jesus Christ
Died for
Tainted
Dung smeared
Sinners
Like me…

He arose with all power in His hand...
So that I could stand...

I'm laced with grace,
A linen of fine flax...
Covered with the Blood of Jesus...
Repented...
And Turned Away...
From Brothel like
Appetites and acts...

With A Foreskin

by Angela Marie
written 7/28/20212 @ 5:15 p.m.

With A Foreskin…
   Thick…
      Insidious…
         And with a flawed smiling face…
           Beholden to a regurgitating vomit
         Is my heart
           When separated from
         God's Grace…

In need of a circumcision
   And that over and over again….
      Because its dank chambers need to be cleansed…

Cut away with a scalpel…
   The flesh
      And its greed…

      For it chases vomit
         And drinks it…
           A backsliding,
           Emotional,
              God hating disease…

The Holy Spirit…
The Blood of Jesus…
The Power of God
   Is what I need…

So cut away the foreskin…
That quiet, but loudly rebellious part of me…

So that my feet can run toward YOU in Holiness…
And live on my knees…

I'd be sensitive to the Very Touch of YOUR Voice…
                         YOUR Presence
                         And the Love YOU Breathe…
                         And Worship YOU in my life…
                                        Inwardly…
                                        Outwardly

Sliding Hooves

by Angela Marie
June 30, 2011 @10:24 AM

Mud
Muddy
Murky
Mud

Hooves
Hind hooves
Holding

Sliding
Unavoidable sliding
Unavoidable slidings

Hooves
Hind hooves
Holding
Sliding
Slipping
Downward
Not able to grasp

So was my heart…
Sliding
Slipping
Downward and away from the things of God…

So was my heart
Feasting
Breathing
Slipping like hind hooves in murky mud…

So was my heart
Ignoring
Avoiding
Time and the Presence of God…

So was my heart
Bleeding
Seething
Slipping
Dying
Wanting
Not reaching
Not reading
Not hearing

The love
The grace
The mercies of God…

So my heart feared
The absence of
The presence
Of God…

I pleaded
I cried…
I sought and heeded the grace and face of God…

His mercies
His mercies
Haulted the sliding hooves of my heart.

I'm vowing…
I'm embracing the mercy and presence of God…
I'm reading
I'm spending time in the Presence of God….

Only He can grab hold of the hind hooves of my heart.
The sliding of my heart
Slipping on murky mud on inclined hills…

To the Utmost
Jesus Saves me.

Taking hold of the hooves of my heart
Slipping on murky mud on inclined hills.

Jesus is the Lord.

Amen

I am Growing

by Angela Marie

I was walking through the market and found myself looking at people as
I sometimes do, because people watching is an amazing thing to do.

And I thought I was fair and kinda nice.

I was perplexed as I began to examine my own thought

Prejudices of my own people
Even based on dialect

And I thought I was fair and kinda nice.

I thought of who was educated and who was not
I was perplexed as I examined my own ill thought

Prejudices planted deep within subconscious thinking
Of which culture within a culture was smart and achieving
And which culture was elite
…the attitude of elitism and its consequences

And I thought I was fair and kinda nice.

My mind looked at attire and its subliminal implication
But it really doesn't indicate finances, ability, or education

I have so many issues and I thought I was fair and kinda nice.

These issues have shown me...
I have to look deep within and carefully examine the thoughts of my
mind like a surgeon
Renew
And refine
My thinking
And cut
And replace
With careful splice

I am growing.

Abrasive Poise

by Angela Marie
Written 3/13/09 @7:45 p.m.

Professional
Black
Degreed
 Degreed
 Degreed

I've forgotten the blemish
Of the brown
 Perfectly smeared upon my face
 But only temporarily

So, I enter the room
 And I speak
 Converse and articulate
 With ease and grace

 But some are in awe of the brown evenly and perfectly
 Airbrushed on my beautiful face…

 But I sense
 Something is wrong
 As I assimilate along

It's not in my mind or imagined as some would believe
    But suddenly my voice is hushed
      I'm blending
        As evaporating steam
       Present
       Warm
        And quietly leaving
        Only droplets
       In the air and
        Nothing more…
         I've been here before

I'm ignored
  And insulted
    With straight faces
     Tactful assumption
      In eloquent conversation

I'd forgotten
Not neglected nor changed
The consciousness of the power of my race
But was abrasively and with poise reminded of my distinguishingly
                       Black
                        Face

A Message To My Brown Skinned Sisters

by Angela Marie
Written July 20, 2009 @ 2:20 PM
<u>Written from a Male perspective</u>

I am a man
And I looked at her.

I admired her beauty
 Wide lips
  And her
   Frame...

I softened her harsh verbal tones
 As our conversation grew
  But anger about a series of past lovers
   Began to spew.
    As time went on
     We engaged in conversation of intellect
      I treated her with mother taught respect.

I was fascinated by her strength
 And everything
  Everything
   But her anger toward her father
    And past lovers
     Caused me to sing...
      Baby baby,
       I didn't hurt you.

I've seen this
    Thrice before…
        A woman that baited
            Me with attached eyelash
                Here verbal abuse arose with flogging punishment
                    Cat-on-nine tails
                        Began to attack.

Her anger toward her past lovers
    And slothful male foe
        Caused me to sing
            Baby Baby, I didn't hurt you.

So, I continued to date women of my race
    Wanting to marry and children create.
        I got tired of canings
            And met a White Woman who treated me with respect.
                I got tired of canings
                    And met a Woman who treated me with Respect.
                        A message to my Brown sisters.

Limited Viewing

by Angela Marie
Written July 20, 2009 @ 8:00

When you look at me
Who or what do you see?

Do you see me
Or my skin only?

When you hear the cadence of my speech
And the tones within my tongue
Do you hear me
Or my dialect
Only?

When you see the texture of my hair
Its kink
Or curl,
What or who do you see
Or is good or bad hair only?

Do you assume my intellect?
Class
My future and past,
Based upon what you hear and see
And is it that a benefit
Or detriment
To me
My family…

Look closer
And
With
Positive objectivity
Perhaps you'll take the time
To get
To
Know
Me
Perhaps you'll like me
maybe

No Apologies

by Angela Marie
Written from a male perspective on 7/18/2009 @10:10 p.m.

I am a man of African American descent
   Born
      And raised
         Saturated
            With the nuances
               Of the culture

Understanding
   The complexities and complexities
      Within
         The
            Race.

So...
   I married the woman with ivory skin,
      On and beneath her face.
We blend our hearts
   And minds
      Our laughter swirls in melodic and dissonant tones...
      Enjoying interlocking bones...

      Doesn't minimize my blackness and the strength of my core
         I'm Black
         I'm Black
         I'm Black
            Can't say it no more...

Their disgust and lynching stares
    Is an infectious, acidic, pus of disgust…
        We try not to care.
        We
            Try
                Not to care.
                    Through hating glares and stares.

My attraction to my Ivory
Is not due to low self esteem.
    The spirit of Ivory
        Is why I married her and queened.

        Doesn't minimize my blackness
            The strength of my core
        The radiance of my brown skinned mother of educated descent.

    Doesn't minimize my struggle
    As an African American.

My attraction to my Ivory is not due to low self esteem
Or white envy
Or a hatred toward my eloquent Black Sisters.

Doesn't minimize my blackness
Or my strength
I married Ivory
Attraction – unforeseen

            Love scent
                Love sent
                    My Queen
                        No Apologies

White Only Beauty

by Angela Marie
Written July 23, 2009 @ 8:55 PM

When I was a girl
Looking at TV
There weren't many girls or families
Colored
Black
Or African American like me

Unless they were poor, struggling or a fatherless entity.

Not too many had hair like mine
Mostly blonde, brunette, refined…

I remember wanting long luxurious locks
Light brown eyes
And light light skin
What were the deeper implications within

I matured and embraced my black beauty
And braid my kinky hair
And enhance my brown pigment
Not desiring to be fair…

But women about 43
With bought blue eyes
And bought blonde wigs
Exhibit effects
Of paraded
Dominant white only

Beauty

One can't escape
The televised and paraded lies about the beauty of our race
Presented in exaggerated
Mammy or
Whorish
Black face

It's my responsibility
To promote a positive self image for my child and those
That surround me

Despite effective divide and conquer, and misinforming strategy.

It is important that our children see the beauty in Me.
And the me I see…

We must continue to overcome the spillage.

We
Are
The
Village

They must listen and learn lessons that speak
The me I see is beautiful.
So that these lessons become a part of their speech of beautiful ebony.
We are beautiful and we must escape,
Segregated
White only beauty in our thinking.

Clear

by Angela Marie Written 7/20/2009 @ 3:23 p.m.

It ain't got no color
It's the spirit of the man that makes him beat me.

It's something controlled
And suffocating inside the child in me that makes me stay.

It ain't got no color
It's the mean spirit in the man that bashes
That gashes
That crumbles my face

It's something ill inside me
Even though I scream
I stay.

It's FEAR
For my life and others.

Superficial speakers don't embrace my Angst

The spirit of the man is unreasonable.
He rapes.

It
Ain't
Got
Nothin'
To
Do
With
Color…

The color of pain
The colors that make me stay.

Thank God
There are no children to see

None
Except me

It ain't got nothing to do with color
'cept the color of pain.
The many colors that make me remain.

Stayin'

by Angela Marie
Written by July 20, 2009 @ 3:03 PM

I've been hurt
Suffered heartache and pain
But I believe in you,
My Black Man...

I see the power of your mind
And hear the goals in your speech
And I rest each time
You hold and squeeze me.

You have insights and I feel
Safe in your presence
And sometimes you really disappoint me
But my love
And commitment to you
Is effervescent,

I'm there.

I'll encourage you
Pray for you
And hold your hand
I'm not goin' anywhere
My Black Man

The ripples in your arm that bulge beneath your brown skin
And your strength within
Draws me.

Even though we sometimes experience strain,
My love for you remains.

I believe in you
My Black Man
And
I ain't goin' nowhere.

I love you
My Black Man
I love you.

From Me to Me

by Angela Marie
written June 22nd, 2015 @ 6:05 p.m.

To the Little Girl inside of me…
Don't worry…
Don't be afraid…
Trust me as I speak…
You will be beautiful…
　　You will be smart…
　　You will be productive…
　　You will be a professional…
　　You will be free…

Free of snarled words hurled at your heart and mind….
　　You will more than survive…
　　　　Trust me as I speak.
　　　　　　You are stronger than you perceive.
　　　　　　　　Christ will carry you when you are weak…

You are a gentle leader even when you cringe inside…
So, trust me as I speak,
　　　Don't worry…
　　　　　Don't be afraid…
　　　　　　Trust what I've seen…
You will accept Jesus as your Lord and Savior and HE will be your
strength…

You will have challenges…
You will make mistakes…
You will have some tears…
But the pain and shame shall soon evaporate…

You will be a wise woman, voluptuous in your curves and words of
poise…
You are a capable, young woman,,,
Trust what I've seen…
And… don't be afraid of you.
And… don't be afraid of them.,,
And don't be afraid to stand…
And don't be afraid to love you.

Don't worry little girl.
Don't worry young woman…
Don't' worry!
You will be alright…
You will be okay….
Trust what I say.
And… don't be afraid of you.
And… don't be afraid of them…And don't be afraid to stand…
And don't be afraid to love you.

Kem's Hair

by Angela Marie

My hair
Thick and beautiful
Young and a part a part of me…
And soooo lovely

My hair
Came out in clumps in my hands and upon my pillow of
Silk
And I cried inside alongside the physical pain.

My hair defined me
And belonged to me

It was leaving my scalp and its roughness revealed
Itself and aged me
And I cried inside alongside
the physical pain.

I wore wigs
And they pained me.

My hair was thick and beautiful
Young and a part of me
And sooo lovely.

And it was leaving me.
And it aged me and left me deformed around the surface of my head.
It left me deformed and bent over inside…

The adolescent boys teased me and
Grabbed hold of the wig

The torture of all my losses and the physical pain
Did
Dig
Dig
Dig.

They taunted and teased
And I cried inside alongside the physical pain.

I cover the mirrors
I can't stand to see
The transformation and pains that plague me.

But I live.
But I live.
And I live.

My hair thick and beautiful
Young and a part of me
And soooo lovely.

And I live without it.
And I live.
And I recover.
My story.

Printed in the United States
By Bookmasters